AMAZON

This edition published 2015 by
Franklin Watts
338 Euston Road
London NW1 3BH

Franklin Watts Australia
Level 17/207 Kent Street
Sydney, NSW 2000

Designed, edited and produced by Paul Manning
Maps by Stefan Chabluk
Proofread and indexed by Alice Harman

Produced for Franklin Watts by
White-Thomson Publishing Ltd

www.wtpub.co.uk
+44 (0) 845 362 8240

A CIP catalogue record for this book is available from
the British Library.

ISBN 978 1 4451 3930 2

Dewey classification: 918.1'1

Key to images

Top cover image: Dense Amazon rainforest
Main cover image: A steamer on the Amazon river
Previous page: An Amazon river dolphin
This page: The Amazon floodplain during the
rainy season.

Note to Teachers and Parents

Every effort has been made to ensure that the websites
listed on page 32 are suitable for children, that they
are of the highest educational value and that they
contain no inappropriate or offensive material. However,
because of the nature of the Internet, it is impossible
to guarantee that the content of these sites will not be
altered. We strongly recommend that Internet access is
supervised by a responsible adult.

Printed in Malaysia

Franklin Watts is a division of Hachette
Children's Books, an Hachette UK company
www.hachette.co.uk

CONTENTS

An Amazon Journey

The Amazon stretches for 6,840 km (4,250 miles). It is the longest river in the world apart from the Nile. Thousands of species live in the river, from piranha fish to pink river dolphin. You will follow the river from its source high in the Andes to its mouth on the eastern coast of Brazil.

A mighty river

The Amazon is so vast that it often seems more like a sea than a river. Its width varies from 1.6 to 10 km (1 to 6.2 miles). In the rainy season, it widens to more than 48 km (30 miles). On its journey, it is joined by hundreds of other rivers called tributaries. Where the Amazon enters the Atlantic Ocean, its estuary measures 240 km (150 miles) across – more than the distance between London and Paris.

The Amazon basin

The area drained by the river is called the Amazon basin. This occupies about 40 per cent of South America. The Amazon basin is covered by tropical rainforest. This forest is one of the richest sources of plant and animal life on Earth.

▲ Together with its tributaries, the Amazon carries more water than any river in the world.

▼ The jaguar is one of millions of animal species found in the Amazon rainforest.

Naming the Amazon

The first European to explore the Amazon was Francisco de Orellana, a Spanish soldier, in 1541-42. Returning from his adventures, Orellana told of fighting with fierce women warriors who lived in the Brazilian jungle. The river was later named 'Amazonas' by the Spanish king Charles V, after the women warriors of Greek mythology.

On map: BRAZIL, Urubamba River, PERU, Lima, Apurímac River, Machu Picchu, ANDES MOUNTAINS, Pacific Ocean

YOU ARE HERE

The High Andes

Your river adventure starts high in the Andes mountains of Peru. Here, the Amazon is fed by many different rivers called headwaters.

The Amazon's source

The Amazon's source is a tiny stream on a volcanic mountain peak called Nevado Mismi. At the foot of a cliff, a simple wooden cross marks the spot where the river begins. Swollen by rain and melted snow, the stream turns into a fast-flowing river. Eventually, it joins the Apurímac River. This joins other rivers which feed into the Amazon further north.

◀ A scientific expedition in 2001 confirmed this spot as the source of the Amazon River.

◀ The city of Machu Picchu is one of the most important surviving relics of the Inca Empire.

An Inca stronghold

The Inca rulers who built Machu Picchu chose the site well. The city is surrounded on three sides by the Urubamba River, a tributary of the Amazon. It is perched on cliffs which rise vertically for 450 m (1,470 ft). The city's location was a closely guarded secret, and the mountains and river around it made it a natural fortress.

The Incas

Centuries ago, the valleys of Amazon tributaries such as the Apurímac and the Urubamba gave food and shelter to people called Incas. The Incas built a great civilization which spread throughout the region. In the 1500s, the Incas were conquered by Spanish soldiers, but many traces of their cities and culture remain.

The most famous Inca site is the city of Machu Picchu. In the 15th century it was the home of the Inca rulers, but was abandoned when the Spanish invaded. In 1911, it was rediscovered by a visiting American historian. Today, it is one of South America's most important historic sites.

▼ Inca craftsmen were skilled metalworkers. This ceremonial mask is made of copper.

YOU ARE HERE

Farming the Andes

In the high Andes valleys, you meet the local people who farm the land. They are known as the Quechua. Many of them are descended from the Incas who once lived here.

▼ This valley was carved by the Urubamba River, a tributary of the Amazon. It was sacred to the Incas because of the fish, water and other resources it provided.

Crop rotation

The Quechua farm the land in the same way as the Incas before them. They grow different crops side by side, and vary them from year to year to allow the soil to recover. They also rear herds of llama and alpaca. They use the wool to make warm clothes to wear in the winter.

◄ Terraces allow crops such as maize to be grown on the sloping valley sides.

Life in the valleys

In prehistoric times, the high Andes valleys were among the earliest places to be inhabited by humans. The valleys gave shelter from the wind and sun, creating cooler temperatures in the daytime and warmer temperatures at night. The first civilizations grew from these river valley communities.

Terraces

On the valley floor, every patch of land is used for growing. On the hillsides, the Quechua farmers have created strips of level land called terraces, so that they can plant more crops. These are supplied with water from the river by channels carved in the rock.

The climate is harsh in the mountains, and it is hard to make a living by farming. Because of this, some Quechuas are beginning to leave the area and move to towns lower down the valley.

► A traditionally dressed Quechua girl with her alpaca.

Amazon Lowlands

YOU ARE HERE

Heading north, you leave the mountains and enter the lowlands of eastern Peru. At Nauta, the rivers Ucayali and Marañón meet, and the main Amazon River begins.

Tropical rainforest

This area is close to the Equator, and the air is hot and sticky. Dense jungle stretches as far as the eye can see. Overhead, the trees form a roof called a canopy. In places, the canopy is so thick that sunlight hardly reaches the ground. This landscape is called tropical rainforest.

It rains here all the year round, and moisture drips constantly from the leaves and branches. The rain swells the river, adding to the flow from the mountains further south.

◀ In the rainforest, tall trees are supported by spreading roots that reach down to collect nutrients from the soil.

Amerindians

People called Amerindians have lived in this region for thousands of years. When Europeans first explored the Amazon basin in the 1500s, about 2 million Amerindians lived here. Today, less than 250,000 are left in the whole of Brazil. Some were killed by foreign invaders. Others were forced to work as slaves on plantations. Many died of diseases brought by European settlers.

Today, the biggest threat to Amerindians is the loss of their land through mining, road-building, cattle-ranching and logging. Some now live in tribal reserves. Here, they can carry on their life and pass on their culture to their children.

▲ These Amerindian children belong to a tribe called the Asháninka.

The Yagua

Yagua people originally came from Peru. They now live in around 30 villages scattered throughout the Peruvian and Colombian Amazon basin. The Yagua live by farming, fishing and hunting. They are skilled at carving animal figures from wood, bone and other materials.

◀ A Yagua tribal elder shows his skill with the blowpipe, a weapon used for hunting.

Iquitos

YOU ARE HERE

About 100 km (62 miles) from Nauta, you reach the city of Iquitos. Over 400,000 people live here. It is the largest city in the world that cannot be reached by road.

▼ Local traders unload a cargo of bananas to sell at Iquitos market. Fish, fruit and vegetables, tobacco and timber are also traded here.

At the riverside, you watch boats unloading their cargoes. The river is a lifeline for Iquitos, and the port and riverside market are always busy. From Iquitos, goods are shipped along the Amazon to other towns up and down the country. This river trade is vital to the city.

▼ A rubber tapper collects latex, the milky white sap that is used to make rubber.

▲ In the rainy season, the Amazon can rise by up to 9 m (30 ft). These homes in Iquitos are built on stilts and floating rafts of balsa wood. This protects them from being flooded.

Natural resources

The land around Iquitos is rich in timber and other natural resources. Natural rubber is collected from the trees in the forest. There are also reserves of oil and gas under the ground. These are sold to other countries, including the USA.

The oil industry has brought money and jobs to the region, but it has also brought pollution. In October 2000, 5,500 barrels of oil spilled into the Marañón river. Fish were poisoned, and many people became ill through drinking contaminated water.

Natural rubber

In the past, the rubber trade brought vast wealth to the cities of the Amazon. Thousands of Amerindians worked as slaves, collecting rubber from trees in the forest, and 'rubber barons' made huge fortunes from their labour. The boom ended with cheap foreign competition, but the rubber industry still continues in the Amazon region.

The Rio Solimões

YOU ARE HERE

At the town of Leticia, you cross the border from Peru into Brazil. Here, the Amazon is known as the Rio Solimões. Much of Brazil's vast rainforest region has never been explored.

▼ Thick rainforest lines the banks of the Brazilian Amazon.

Navigating the river

Travelling through the rainforest by road is very difficult, and so the river is a vital transport route. From time to time, you pass local traders, using small boats and dugout canoes to take their wares to market. You also see rafts and barges transporting heavier goods, such as timber, out of the forest.

◄ In its middle course, the Amazon flows in giant loops called meanders.

Meanders

A meander is formed when a river washes away stones and mud on the outside of a bend and drops it on the opposite bank. Over time, this gradually causes the bend to widen. Sometimes, the bend becomes so wide that the river joins up with itself further downstream. When this happens, a horseshoe-shaped 'oxbow lake' is formed, away from the main river.

River creatures

As you make your way downriver, your guide points out a pair of manatees in the water. These gentle seal-like creatures can grow up to 3 m (10 ft) long, but are shy and rarely seen. The river is also home to turtles, alligators, lizards, river dolphins and thousands of fish species, from giant pirarucu to flesh-eating piranhas.

▶ Manatees are sometimes known as 'sea cows'. They are usually found in shallow, slow-moving waters.

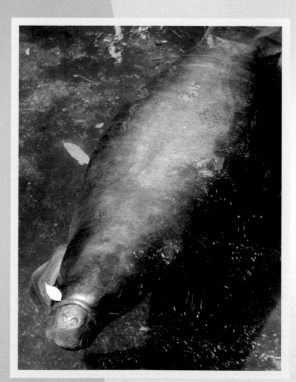

Life on the River

YOU ARE HERE

Deep in the rainforest, you pass a remote village by the river. The people who live here are far away from the nearest town. They rely on the river and the land around them for food and shelter.

▶ Fish from the river is a vital food for people living by the Amazon.

Hunting and gathering

In the past, the rainforest was inhabited by Amerindian tribes who lived entirely by hunting and gathering. The Amerindians caught fish from the river and boiled it in pots or smoked it over a fire to preserve it. Animals were hunted with bows and arrows or killed with darts tipped with a poison found in the rainforest, called curare.

◄ Amerindian children enjoy a meal of freshly caught fish cooked over a wood fire.

Subsistence farming

Today, most of the people who occupy forest land are subsistence farmers. They grow crops like manioc and rice on small plots of land, producing just enough to feed their families. After a time, the heavy rains wash the minerals from the soil. When the soil becomes infertile, the farmers move on.

Over time, this type of farming, known as 'shifting cultivation', harms the environment. Many blame the Brazilian government for encouraging too many people to settle on land that is not really suitable for farming.

Rainforest medicines

Plants that grow in the rainforest often have healing properties, and many plant remedies have been used by Amerindians for generations. The US National Cancer Institute has identified over 3,000 plant species that help destroy cancer cells. Of these, around 75 per cent are found in the Amazon rainforest,

▶ As well as giving us chocolate, cocoa from the Amazon has been shown to reduce the risk of cancer, heart disease and stroke.

The Várzea

YOU ARE HERE

From November to June each year, the Amazon is swollen by heavy rains, and land on either side of the river is flooded. The area affected by the flood is called the 'várzea', or 'flooded forest'.

▼ The Amazon floodplain, known as the várzea, has some of the most fertile farmland in the Amazon basin.

Feeding the floodplain

The Amazon flood is vital to the region. As the river spreads across the floodplain, it brings rich sediment called silt that turns the water a muddy brown. When the flood waters retreat, silt is left behind to enrich the soil. The rest of the silt is carried to the river's mouth, known as its delta.

◄ During the rainy season, forest in the várzea is flooded. Sometimes, trees are completely submerged and fish swim among the branches.

Farming the floodplain

The people of the várzea use the river to help them farm the land. They build low banks of earth which trap the floodwater and prevent it draining back into the river. This water is used to irrigate crops during the dry season. The water sinks slowly into the soil, leaving silt that helps the crops to grow. This method is called basin irrigation.

Harvesting manioc

One of the most important crops grown in the várzea is manioc. When the manioc roots are big, farmers dig them up, peel them and boil them to make a pulp. They squeeze the liquid out to get rid of poisons. The pulp is dried, then pounded into flour and used to make bread.

► A farmer and his family make farinha, a staple Brazilian food made from manioc roots.

YOU ARE HERE

Where Rivers Meet

South of Manaus, the Amazon is joined by its biggest tributary – the Rio Negro, or 'black river'. The point where the rivers meet is called their confluence.

The Rio Negro

The Rio Negro's source is 2,400 km (1,500 miles) north-west, in the highlands of Colombia. Its dark colour comes from the rotting leaves it picks up from the rainforest on its journey. The Amazon gets its milky colour from the sediment it brings down from the Andes. For 80 km (50 miles), the two rivers flow side by side before finally merging.

▼ This huge road bridge is being built across the Rio Negro at Manaus.

◄ The lighter-coloured waters of the Amazon meet the Rio Negro at Manaus.

Hydropower

The Amazon carries more water than any other river system on Earth. As well as helping to irrigate fields and grow crops, this water is used to generate electricity.

Since the 1970s, giant hydroelectric dams have been built on rivers throughout the Amazon basin. Supporters argue that the energy they supply is important for Brazil's economy, but many believe there are better ways to solve the country's energy needs. Because of fierce opposition from environmentalists and local people, many dam projects have recently been halted.

Victims of the dams

Hydroelectric dams in the Amazon have wiped out plant and animal species, flooded wetlands and displaced thousands of people. Campaigners are now working with local communities and with Brazil's government to make sure that future projects safeguard the environment and respect the wishes of local people.

▶ When large-scale dams are built, land has to be flooded to make way for reservoirs. This often harms local communities.

21

BRAZIL

Rio Negro

Manaus

Amazon River

Purus River

Madeira River

YOU ARE HERE

▼ *Amazon steamers unload goods and passengers at Manaus port.*

On the north bank of the Rio Negro is Manaus. This is the biggest city in the Amazon basin. It is home to nearly 2 million people.

The 'Heart of the Amazon'

Manaus started as a fort built by Portuguese settlers. Today, it is the region's most important commercial and industrial centre. From here, ocean-going ships and cruise liners sail all the way down to the river's mouth. Although it has an airport, Manaus is very isolated by road, and has no rail links to other cities. The river is its most important link with the outside world.

◀ The Teatro Amazonica opera house in Manaus was built with money from the rubber trade.

Local industries

Like Iquitos, Manaus became wealthy at the beginning of the last century from the trade in natural rubber. Steamboats carried the rubber downriver. From the coastal port of Belém, it was exported all over the world.

Today, rubber is still collected from the forest, but other industries are more important. Big mobile phone companies such as Nokia have factories here. Oil is brought to the city to be turned into petrol. Manaus is also a growing centre for river cruises and eco-tourism.

Eco-tourism

Many visitors now come to see the scenery and wildlife of the Amazon basin. 'Eco-tourists' stay in simple wooden lodges in the rainforest, and learn about the area with the help of local guides. Because numbers are limited, visitors can enjoy being close to nature without harming the environment.

▶ On organised eco-tours, visitors can see the Amazon and its wildlife at close quarters.

YOU ARE HERE

The Lower Amazon

As you travel the lower Amazon, you can see the dramatic changes that have taken place here. Huge areas of rainforest have been cleared to make way for large-scale farming and industry.

Roads, logging and mining

In the past, plants, animals and humans lived together here in a delicate balance. When the trees were cut down, plant and animal habitats were lost, and the balance was destroyed.

Since the 1980s, more than 10,000 km (6,200 miles) of new roads have been driven through the Amazon rainforest. Indigenous people have been driven from their land by gangs of illegal loggers. Mining companies have moved in, and waste material from mines and industrial plants has drained into rivers and poisoned the fish.

◀ A new highway carves its way through what was once unspoilt rainforest.

◀ Many former forest areas are now occupied by cattle ranches. Beef from these ranches is sold to countries all over the world.

Protecting the rainforest

Today, the rate of deforestation is slowing. There are signs that the Brazilian government is finally acting to protect the rainforest.

Plans have been announced to divide the forest into zones, and to limit cattle-ranching to areas where wildlife is not endangered. New areas of forest will be planted, and mining and logging companies will have to plant trees on land that they have previously cleared. As the new forests grow, they will provide habitats for animals, and wildlife will gradually be encouraged to return to the area.

▶ These saplings will be planted in areas of the Amazon that have been deforested.

Tropical hardwood

In the past, one of the main causes of deforestation was the cutting down of hardwood trees for export. Today, there are strict laws on the sale of hardwoods, and all timber must come from renewable sources. For every tree that is cut down, another has to be planted in its place.

The Amazon Delta

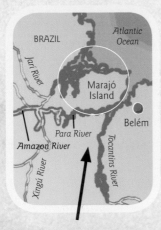

YOU ARE HERE

As you approach the Amazon Delta, the river splits into many channels which weave their way through islands of silt. These islands are constantly shifting as silt is built up and washed away by the action of the river.

Marajó Island

▼ During the rainy season, grazing land on Marajó Island is flooded.

Marajó is the largest island in the delta. It covers an area the size of Switzerland. Two thousand years ago, it was occupied by Arua Indians. Today, the island is almost entirely populated by herds of water buffalo *(below)* that graze in the marshy pastureland. According to local legend, the buffalo first arrived here after being shipwrecked in the delta.

▲ These wooded
islands are made
of silt dropped
by the river.

Where river meets sea

Beyond Marajó Island, the river finally
reaches the sea. But even here its journey
is not over. The current is so strong that
it pushes the river hundreds of kilometres
into the Atlantic, forming a plume
of lighter-coloured
water. It was the
sight of this river
water so far out
to sea that first led
Spanish explorers to
the Amazon 500
years ago.

▶ This Arua Indian vase
was made some time
between 1400 and
400 BCE.

Clay from the river

*The Arua Indians who once
lived on Marajó Island were
skilled potters. They used clay
from the riverbank to make
beautifully decorated vases,
which they left to bake hard
in the sun. Potters on Marajó
Island still make fine
vases today.*

YOU ARE HERE

Journey's End

At the city of Belém, the Amazon is joined by the Tocantins River. Here you reach the end of your Amazon adventure.

▼ Cargo and ferry boats line the harbour at Belém. On the quayside behind is a market selling goods from all over the Amazon region.

Belém was originally built as a fort by Portuguese settlers to defend their territory from other European invaders. It later became a centre of the slave trade. Many of the people here are descended from slaves brought from Africa three centuries ago to work on plantations in the Amazon basin.

◀ An Amazon river steamer approaches the modern city of Belém.

A busy port

Because of its location at the river mouth, Belém was vital to the Portuguese traders. From here, ships would head across the Atlantic with cargoes of spices, coffee, tobacco and sugar. Other ships sailed upriver, bringing supplies to the settlements on the banks of the Amazon.

Today, more than 2 million people live in Belém, and all kinds of goods pass through its port. Timber is one of Brazil's biggest exports, and more than 20 million cubic tonnes are shipped abroad from Belém each year.

A tasty fruit

The tasty açaí fruit sold in Belém are a good example of a crop that can be produced without harming the environment. The fruit comes from a palm tree that grows on islands in the Amazon delta. The leaves of the palm are also used to make hats, mats, baskets and thatch for roofing.

▶ A trader sells açaí fruit on the quayside at Belém.

Glossary

blowpipe a weapon made from a hollow tube of wood that is used to shoot darts

canopy the top layer of foliage in a rainforest

confluence the point where two rivers meet

contaminated dirty or infected

delta the area at the mouth of a river where silt is deposited

displace to drive out

dugout canoe a canoe made from the hollowed-out trunk of a tree

enrich to feed or nourish

estuary the place where a river widens and flows into the sea

floodplain the area affected by a river's floodwaters

habitat the natural home of a plant or animal

headwater the source of the water in a river or stream

hydropower energy produced from fast-flowing water

indigenous peoples the original inhabitants of a country or region

irrigate to supply water to a field in order to grow crops

logging cutting down trees for timber

meander a pattern of loops or bends formed by a river

natural resources materials that come directly from the natural environment

nutrient a source of food or nourishment

pastureland an area where cattle graze

plantation a large farm for growing a single crop

plume a long spreading shape that narrows at one end

prehistoric before records began

pulp a mushy substance

ranch a large farm for rearing cattle or sheep

sacred precious, holy

sapling a young tree

sediment broken down stones and mud from the riverbed

shoal a number of fish swimming together

silt fine sediment carried downstream by a river

slave someone who is 'owned' by another person and forced to work in cruel and inhuman conditions

species a type of plant or creature

spice a plant extract used to flavour or preserve food

stilt a length of timber used to raise a hut or house off the ground

submerge to swallow up or cover

subsistence farming growing just enough food to eat

thatch a material used for covering a roof

tributary a river or stream that flows into another, bigger one

wetland an area where the soil is waterlogged for all or part of the year

Amazon Quiz*

Find the answers in this book, or look them up online.

1 Match the captions to the pictures.

A A piranha fish

B Manioc roots

C An açaí palm

D An Amazon
     steamboat

E A heliconia plant

F A toucan

2 These places can all be found along the Amazon. Place them in the right order, starting with the ones nearest to the sea:

Iquitos
Belém
Leticia
Manaus
Nauta
Santarém

4 This man is working by the banks of the Amazon. What is he doing?

3 True or false?

'There are no bridges over the Amazon.'

*Answers on page 32.

Websites and Further Reading

Websites

- *http://kids.nationalgeographic.com/explore/countries/brazil/*
A good short introduction to Brazil.

- *www.rainforesteducation.com medicines/PlantMedicines/rfmedicines.htm*
An interesting short guide to plant medicines used by rainforest peoples.

- *http://gowild.wwf.org.uk/americas*
Fact files, stories, games and activities focusing on the Amazon rainforest.

Further reading

Brazil and Rio de Janeiro (Developing World series) by Louise Spilsbury (Franklin Watts, 2013)

The Amazon ('Journey Along a River' series), Jen Green (Wayland, 2009)

Brazil ('Changing World' series), Nicola Barber (Franklin Watts, 2010)

Index

Answers to Amazon Quiz
1 1D, 2C, 3A, 4E, 5F, 6B. **2** Belém, Santarém, Manaus, Leticia, Iquitos, Nauta. **3** True. The river mostly flows through tropical rainforest where there are very few roads or cities. There is therefore no need for crossings. **4** He is searching (panning) for gold in the riverbed.